I0472929

# Sales Is
# Mashed Potatoes

## Other Motivational Books
## By Tim Northburg

Decide On It!

Fuel The Furnace

Fuel The Furnace
Workbook

Otterocity!

Otterocity!
Field Guide

Realize It!

Realize It!
Goals Workbook

# Sales Is Mashed Potatoes

A Pocket Guide To Keep
You Motivated In Sales

Tim Northburg

# Sales Is Mashed Potatoes

Copyright © 2012 Tim Northburg. All rights reserved.

Published by Tim Northburg and LifeWork Elements

No part of this publication may be reproduced, stored in a retrieval system or transmitted in any form or by any means electronic, mechanical, photocopying, recording, scanning or otherwise, except as permitted under Section 107 or 108 of the 1976 United States Copyright Act, without wither the prior written permission of the Publisher, or authorization through payment of the appropriate per-copy fee. Requests for permission should be emailed to Tim Northburg, LifeWork Elements at lifeworkelements@gmail.com, or visit us online at www.lifeworkelements.com

Limit of Liability/Disclaimer of Warranty: While the publisher and author have used their best efforts in preparing this book, they make no representations or warranties with respect to the accuracy or completeness of the contents of this book and specifically disclaim any implied warranties of merchantability or fitness for a particular purpose. No warranty may be created or extended by sales representatives or written sales materials. The advice and strategies contained herein may not be suitable for your situation. You should consult with a professional where appropriate. Neither the publisher nor author shall be liable for any loss of profit or any other commercial damages, including but not limited to special, incidental, consequential, or other damages.

ISBN: 1470067145

ISBN-13: 978-1470067144

Sales Is Mashed Potatoes

# Contents

## Sales Is Mashed Potatoes

*"A month's worth of sales is like mashed potatoes. Every day you dig up potatoes; large potatoes, medium potatoes, and small potatoes. At the end of the month, you boil them up and mash them together, and what do you have?"*

*"A big pot of mashed potatoes!"*

—Doug Axtell

# Dedication

This book is dedicated to my good friend and mentor, Doug Axtell. You taught me a lot about setting goals, having persistence, following processes, and how to become successful. You also taught me that sales is mashed potatoes and you helped me become a great potato digger. Thanks!

Doug Axtell
1950-2009

# Key

When reading this book remember:

Sales = Potatoes
Deals = Potatoes
Transactions = Potatoes
Customers = Potatoes
Prospects = Potatoes
Clients = Potatoes
Your Product = Potatoes
Salesperson = Digger
Sales Manager = Digger
Employees = Diggers
Your Business = Farm
Problems = Warts
Challenges = Blight

# Preface

From an early age, I was always inclined to sell things. In Junior High School, I took my lunch money to the grocery store and bought a twelve pack of chewing gum before school. I would sell my packs of gum to my friends and other students in the halls. I doubled my money and was able to buy an extra dessert or a second entree at lunch. I would get some more gum the next day and do it all over again.

In 1994, I started selling life and health insurance. I received my Series 6 Investment license, and worked as a Financial Planner. I did an okay job, sold some insurance and set up several mutual fund accounts. But, at 22 I found it hard to get older clients to trust my financial planning abilities.

My step dad worked in a car dealership, that his father was part owner. He told me that car sales was a lucrative career for him and that I would do well in it.

Then, in 1996, I decided to move to automotive sales. After working in the automotive business for six months, I felt I wanted something more. I, like other sales people, was always on the lookout for that 'big potato.'

I went to work for Saturn; a different kind of car company that focused on customer service. I started steady in sales, worked my way to top salesperson, and I got more potatoes than I could imagine. In 1999, I became salesperson of the year and had a 98% customer satisfaction rating from my customers.

In 2000, I became a Sales Manager. I was in charge of running our Business Development Center and worked car deals as a backup manager.

One day, my boss Doug Axtell and I were talking. I asked him what I needed to do to be a successful manager.

He looked me straight in the eye and told me, "A month's worth of sales is like mashed potatoes. Every day you dig up potatoes; large potatoes, medium potatoes, and small potatoes. At the end of the month, you boil them up and mash them together, and what do you have?"

"What?" I asked.

# Sales Is Mashed Potatoes

"A big pot of mashed potatoes!"

I looked at him sideways.

"You need to get all the potatoes you can—even the small ones."

From that day on, it stuck in my head. It didn't take long for me to understand what he meant. Despite the size of gross profit, you have to take all the deals you can get—they all add up. It is about taking as many deals you can get (big, medium, or small) because in the end, the more customers you make, the more customers you will be able to retain. The more customers you retain, the more you have to nurture for repeat and referral business.

In my management career, I took his saying to heart. I did my best to get as many potatoes as I could—all sizes!

As a manager today, I try to continue getting as many potatoes as possible and do my best to instill this in the sales people I lead.

That is why I am sharing these thoughts about potatoes with you. I hope you can become the best you can.

Please enjoy.

# Sales Is Mashed Potatoes

# Introduction

All over the world, there are fertile fields of dirt that grow potatoes. These potatoes are the driving force of life. They provide a living for all those who dig them up.

There are all kinds of potatoes out there; fat ones, big ones, thin ones, and tiny ones. Unless you are looking for them, you won't find them.

If you are a potato digger, (in sales, either a salesperson or manager) you want to find these potatoes—they are your livelihood. All you have to do is find them and get them into your sack. But, it is not that easy. Many are covered in dirt—and it is back breaking work uncovering them.

It takes a rare person to be a potato digger. You have to have tenacity, persistence, hard work, skill, and a bit of luck.

Many times, you want to give up. You may want to quit because you haven't harvested any potatoes lately. Your back may hurt from constantly bending over all the time. But, no matter, you keep sifting through the dirt finding more potatoes.

Once you have enough, you take your potatoes home, wash them off, peel their skin, cut them up, and throw them into a pot to boil. After they are good and soft, you drain them off and mash them up with a little milk and butter. Then, you and your family enjoy a big pot of creamy mashed potatoes.

The next morning you get up, put on your digging clothes and boots to do it all over again. That is what you were born to do—be a potato digger and make mashed potatoes.

# Becoming A Potato Digger

So, you decided to get into sales. You are a people person. You want to have fun and you like the opportunity to be able to tap into an unlimited wealth—the sales fields are fertile and produce an abundance of sustenance. You chose a product to sell and you now call yourself a salesperson.

It is your first day. Hopping out of bed, you are excited. You eat a good breakfast, brush your teeth and get ready to get on with the day.

You put on your suit, or uniform, and make your way to your sales position. When you arrive at your office, or building, you manager has a surprise for you.

He hands you overalls, boots, gloves and a shovel and he tells you to get digging?

"Digging for what?" you ask.

# Sales Is Mashed Potatoes

"Potatoes." he replies

"Potatoes? Are you serious?"

"Yes, potatoes. You see, you are not a sales person—you're a potato digger."

"Potato digger? I thought I was sales person."

He nods and tells you, "In order to be a successful sales person you have to be a great potato digger. You see sales = potatoes. You just have to find the potatoes."

Potatoes are everywhere around you; big ones, medium ones, and small ones. They are strolling down the street, walking through the doors of your business, calling on the phones, and clicking away on the internet.

You think it would be simple work digging potatoes. Oh, it's fun being a potato digger. There is nothing in the world that's more exciting and exhilarating. The truth is, it is very hard work. Many before you have tried and failed. Potato digging is not for everyone. If it were simple, everyone would be doing it.

In order to be a successful potato digger there are some things you should know. You need to know where to look for potatoes and which fields are the best. You need to know how to dig and where to dig. You need to know how to handle blight, pests, and other challenges.

## Sales Is Mashed Potatoes

Once you know how to dig potatoes and establish yourself as a potato digger, you can do it anywhere.

Do you want to become a potato digger? Are you going to, "Give it at try?"

Don't give it a try. It is what you were born to do. It's time to put indecision behind you and "do it" fully. Be 100% committed to digging potatoes. There is no *try* in life, there is only *do*!

Declare yourself to be the best darn potato digger ever and go out there and make it happen!

# Potato Digging Tools

Be prepared. Make sure you have all the tools ready to do your job. A construction worker doesn't go to work without a hammer, or his tool box. A doctor doesn't go to work without his stethoscope. A Lawyer doesn't go to work without his case files. Why would you go to work without your tools?

It happens every day. Potato diggers go to work unprepared and not ready to dig.

The secret to becoming a successful potato digger is preparedness. Here are some things you should do to be ready to dig potatoes:

**Get up early.** Does the farmer sleep in until noon? Does the rancher wait until midday to let his cattle out to pasture? Not on a working day. Neither should a potato digger. Start your day off right. Get up early, eat a good breakfast, and drink some milk, juice, or coffee. Take a nice hot shower and prepare yourself for a full day of potato digging. If you get up late, and are dragging all day, you are not going to be a very effective potato digger. If your body is sluggish—your mind will follow sut.

**Fuel your body, fuel your mind.** Not only is it important to have a good breakfast, eat the proper lunch, and have a nourishing dinner, you need to fuel your mind. Knowledge is power. It is the fuel of success. Learn from other potato diggers. Go to potato conventions or potato training camps. Learn the act of better, smarter digging. Find new ways to grow healthier potatoes and discover new tactics for harvesting more potatoes.

**Prepare your tools.** A great potato digger takes care of their equipment. The tractor has to be maintained. Boots need to be clean and dry with no holes in them. The shovels and spades need to be sharp and in good working order with no broken handles or cracked shafts.

You have to have the proper tools. You can't go digging for potatoes with a fork and spoon. (Okay, you can but it would take you forever.) That being said, as a potato digger, having your tools in tiptop shape will make you job a whole lot easier and you will be more productive. Make sure you have the right tools in order to do your job.

# Sales Is Mashed Potatoes

**Always be on the lookout.** An expert potato digger is always on the lookout for fertile fields to dig in. Be constantly prospecting for potatoes. They are lurking under the dirt and rocks; at the grocery store, the coffee shop, the bank, the gas station, or wherever your market is. Be ready to dig at any given moment. Don't be afraid to get dirty. Don't hesitate to dig, or your potatoes will spoil.

**Believe in yourself.** To harvest more potatoes and make a ton of mashed potatoes you have to believe you can do it. Believe with your whole heart, mind, and body that you can be a successful potato digger.

When you dig your fist potato and put it in your bag you will feel an excitement like nothing ever before. It is that joy and thrill of success that keeps you coming back day after day—to dig more potatoes. It is the excitement of not knowing what you are going to find next. What shape is it going to be? How big is it going to be?

That thrill and enjoyment for what you do will build belief in yourself. It is that feeling inside that will fuel yourself and push you to your success. Keep it going. Don't give up and never, ever lose the joy for digging potatoes—if you do, it is time to hang up your hat and find a different career.

## Sales Is Mashed Potatoes

Without all of these things, you will not be an excellent potato digger. Before you do anything else, make sure you have the right tools and mind-set to make this a lucrative career. You can become a mashed potato mogul—it's all up to you.

# Don't Focus On One Potato

Just think of an award winning one hundred pound potato. How nice would that one potato be? It could feed many people.

It all sounds nice, but if you spend all of your time nurturing that one potato, waiting for it to grow to the perfect size you may pull the behemoth out of the ground and find out that it is inedible. You spent all that time and energy on that one large potato and it is not any good.

What are you going to do then? With all the time you spent on that one massive potato, the other potatoes will be gone. Other diggers will have dug them up and the rest will have rot.

Yes, that one potato may pay off huge for you and you will look like a hero if it pans out. Many times I have seen potato diggers focusing on that one great big potato and it

Sales Is Mashed Potatoes

doesn't pay off. In the mean time, they have
failed to see the little ones and they end up
with nothing.

Good potato diggers are not nearsighted;
they don't focus only on one potato. They
don't just see at a short distance and only look
at what's in front of them. They see the whole
field.

When you are bent over digging; focusing
at that one big potato, remember there is a big
field out there. Let alone, there are many fields
out there with all kinds and sized of potatoes.

Does that mean you can't be on the
lookout for that one massively grand potato
that will feed you and everyone? No.

Great potato diggers know there are more
where they come from, and there are all kinds
of potatoes too but they also know when they
are trying to do too much at one time. Be
careful not to spread yourself too thin.

Here are a few other things to focus your
attention on:

**Set Goals.** You can't make it big or build
an empire overnight. Set goals for yourself.
Have short, intermediate, and long-term goals.
Start with one small plot of land to dig potatoes
from and monitor your progress as you go. As
you gain success, add more land. Increase that
plot to an acre, then multiple acres. Soon

enough, you will have several fertile fields you are working.

**Discipline yourself.** It is not all about digging. Before you dig anything up you have to till your land and get the dirt ready for planting. After you plant, you have to weed, and irrigate your land. As your tubers grow, you have to mitigate pests and weather any storms. All this takes time and patience. In addition, patience takes discipline. Ready yourself for the digging season.

**Always move.** Do you ever see a successful potato digger sitting and staring at the land? No. They are constantly moving, constantly doing. There is a lot to do around the potato farm. When you are in-between digs, make sure you are doing the right things to prepare yourself and ensure a successful dig. If you don't plant, weed, feed, and mitigate you won't have anything to dig up. Remember, activity breeds more activity. If you are constantly moving, you may just bump into that big potato you have been looking for.

**Moderate yourself.** Moderation is key to success. You can go all out and plant a whole bunch of fields of potatoes and have a successful dig, but be careful. If you plant too many fields, you won't be able to tend to all of the potatoes. Plant too few fields and you won't have enough to live off of. Don't burn yourself out, and don't starve yourself out either.

As you can see, there is a lot you can focus on—or you can just concentrate on that one massive potato. It is up to you what kind of success you want to have digging.

Just remember, successful mashed potato moguls don't focus on that one potato.

# Don't Judge A Potato
# By Its Jacket

As the saying goes, "Don't judge a book by its cover!" so too goes, "Don't judge a potato by its jacket!"

When you pull a potato out of a deep dark hole and its wrinkled, has a tough skin, and looks dark brown and unsavory—on the outside it looks unworthy of being put in your bag—what do you do?

This time you decide to take it home.

At home, you wash it off and bake it. When it is done you, cut it open and find out that under the rough "potato jacket" exterior is a soft, sweet inside that is light and fluffy and melts in your mouth.

Maybe, you take it and peel away the tough skin, slice it up, and with a bit of oil you roast the pieces of fine potato flesh. After a bit, you pull them out and you have nice crispy potato bites that are so scrumptious.

Or, you peel that same potato and add it to the others in the boiling pot. You add some butter, milk, and a touch of garlic and it is so tasty.

The point is . . . there are so many times you look at a potato and think it isn't any good and toss it over your shoulder. If you had not gone with your pre-conceived notions and done some investigating, you would have seen that it was a good potato on the inside after all.

Don't pass up a potato because it doesn't look good on the outside. It may just surprise you and be good after all.

# No Potato Is
# The Same

Potatoes come in different sizes. Like size, each potato has its own shape. Some are smooth, some are knobby, and some have eyes or things growing out of them.

There are all kinds of potatoes—an upwards of over 4000 different varieties. There are Russett, Burbank, Yukon Gold, Red Bliss, New, Fingerlings, Sweet, Blue, and more.

Potatoes are all over the world. Some top producing countries are; People's Republic of China, India, Russia, the United States, Germany, France, and the Netherlands.

The world is culturally diverse. Potatoes are an intricate part of the world's cuisine. Even our country is comprised of many different regions of potatoes with different categories. Some are all-purpose, waxy, or starchy.

## Sales Is Mashed Potatoes

You have to remember each potato is different. Don't throw away a potato because you don't like its shape or size. All shapes and sizes are useful. When they are mashed up do you remember what size or shape they were? No. You know that you have a whole lot of mashed potatoes.

On top of that, don't just focus on one kind of potato to make your living. Just because you have a preference for one type of potato doesn't mean others are any less significant. Be aware of the diverseness of your potatoes and understand their unique differences.

All-Purpose potatoes are good for most anything. Waxy ones are smooth, and somewhat tougher in texture. Starchy potatoes are the best for mashing because they don't hold up well when cooked but be careful not to over work them or they will become a gluey mess.

Understanding your potatoes will help you establish yourself as a professional potato digger.

Successful potato diggers are aware of the diverse potato market. They are respectful and sensitive to the various potato types.

Don't be selective, all potatoes provide food and a living. Remember, potatoes vary and each one is unique.

# A Small Potato Is Better Than No Potato

Many people scoff at the small potatoes. They don't think they are worth their time or effort.

Only the greedy solely go after the big potatoes. What happens if no big ones grow? You will be left with nothing.

A successful potato digger would rather take a small potato than a rotten one or a big one with brown spots. Put several small, good quality potatoes together and you can make a meal of them.

You see, potato digging is what you make it. It all comes down to the attitude you have towards your potatoes. Be positive about the small potatoes. Tell yourself that you are going to take all the potatoes you can, regardless of size. Be just as excited to dig up a small or medium size potato, as the large ones. Just because it is small doesn't mean that it won't provide you with sustenance, or a good living. They aren't any less significant than the big ones. In fact, you can make a lot of mashed potatoes with lots of small potatoes.

Tell me of a potato digger that would rather have no potatoes at all over several small potatoes.

You would be a fool to think that the small potatoes are unworthy of your attention.

Just hang up your shovel, if you do.

# Potatoes Lead
# To Other Potatoes

More often than not, big, medium, and small potatoes lead to other potatoes. Those potatoes will tell you where other potatoes are.

However, big potatoes are less likely to lead to more potatoes. The big potatoes that you made a killing on usually don't grow back. They may find from others that the deal they got was not at all good. They might feel ripped off or taken advantage of. So, they don't return, they also don't recommend you to other potatoes.

Medium and small size potatoes are your bread and butter. They usually get a good deal, are happy, and will tell other potatoes about their experience.

The teeny-tiny potatoes, don't generate much profits, and can be somewhat needy. They are small and want all the attention. But they still come back and tell others. You have to determine if they are worth the time and effort into peeling them and adding them to your pot of mashed potatoes.

Take care of your potatoes. Nurture them and follow-up with them because all sizes of potatoes go into building a network of more potatoes. If they are happy potatoes, they will come back and refer other potatoes to you.

If you can get 100 or 1000 potatoes out there rounding up their friends, family, and co-workers to join them in your fields and ultimately ending up in your pot, it will make your job easier. Even the teeny-tiny ones have other potatoes they know. A good referral base is more powerful than conquesting unknown fields. It takes less time and it costs less money.

Don't get me wrong, you need new fields, but your harvest will be ten-fold with repeat and referral potatoes.

# Big Potatoes Get Brown Spots Too

You dig up a nice big potato. It looks great on the outside but when you cut into it, there are brown spots everywhere. You find out it is no good.

Just because a potato is big doesn't mean it isn't prone to developing brown spots. Large potatoes aren't always good.

Sometimes you may spend a lot of time digging out one potato. It might be a bugger to get out, sandwiched between two rocks or deep down in the ground.

It looks nice on the outside, then you find out it is full of brown spots. What did you spend all that time on?

If a potato is rude, high maintenance, demanding, you have to decide if it is worth your time digging out a large potato with brown spots.

## Sales Is Mashed Potatoes

Sometimes it is worth it. It turns out all right when you cut away the brown.

Sometimes it isn't worth it. You have nothing left when you chop away the brown.

It is okay to throw a potato back. Just because you dig it up doesn't mean you have to put it in your sack.

Just remember—you are doing the digging. It is your decision if the degree of difficulty is worth the effort of pulling the potato out with brown spots. Only you can decide what potato you are going to take.

Just remember, the big potatoes get brown spots too.

# A Potato Is
# Just A Potato

A potato is just a potato. Experienced potato diggers know this. When they dig up a potato that is no good, spoiled, or rotten they toss it away and move on.

To them, it's no big deal if they don't get a potato right there and then. They don't stress out over potato digging. Successful potato diggers know to move on and find the next potato. They keep on going because there are more out there. They don't get discouraged—they can sense them in the dirt.

Also, don't hold onto the potatoes you have or they will shrivel and go bad. Problems come when you hoard the potatoes you have. Sell them, or mash them up and eat them while they are good. If you think they are the only ones you are going to get, you panic. When you panic, you become irrational. When you are irrational, you make bad business decisions. Don't forget there are more potatoes out there where they came from.

On top of that, too many times you may get distracted looking at other people's potatoes. You begin to get jealous and think, "Am I going to get one that big?" or "Wow, they have a lot of potatoes." When you do this, you fail to take the potatoes at your feet. Don't worry about other potato diggers. Just focus on your task at hand—digging out as many potatoes as you can to make a good living for yourself.

Many times, there are potato diggers out there who rant and rave, yell and scream. They may be angry that they didn't get enough potatoes, jealous over the potatoes you are getting, or they have been digging potatoes too long and have become cynical and bitter about the business. It doesn't help them get any more potatoes. Don't become like them.

If you find yourself angry or jealous, you may need to figure out what is wrong with your digging processes. If you become bitter or cynical, maybe you need to find a renewed enthusiasm for what you are doing—or find another profession all together.

In addition to this, don't ever discredit the potatoes in front of you. Potatoes don't like it when they are ignored or treated disrespectfully—especially in front of other potatoes. If a potato isn't worthy to put in your bag (for credit issues or other reasons) plant it back into the ground and come back to it later. It may surprise you and turn into a nice big potato.

Remember a potato is just a potato. It's no biggie. That doesn't mean you should not take your potato digging seriously, but you shouldn't get frustrated to the point where it hurts your attitude and mental fortitude. You should however, get frustrated to the point that sparks change and instigates action. For what it's worth, getting worked up over potato digging is destructive behavior.

I am going to say it again . . . it's no biggie, it's just a potato.

# Keys To Getting More Potatoes

When you run out of potatoes, and trust me there will be a point in your digging career where you will run out of potatoes, you have to be ready to take that next potato. Preparedness is the answer to all digging woes, but here are a few keys to getting more potatoes.

**Prospect for more.** Dig in new ground and turn over rocks to find those hiding from you. While you are doing that, work your referral potato base. Referrals will tell you where to look for more potatoes. Sometimes potatoes just appear—the rain washes the soil away revealing new potatoes. Other times potatoes find you—via the phone and internet.

**Replant.** There will be a time where you have to take a step back, re-plant, and wait for more potatoes to grow.

**Take care of yourself.** Rest between seasons or between digs. A happy mind = happy body = happy digging.

**Follow a Routine.** Make sure you are doing the things necessary, on a daily basis, for you to be successful. This means sharpening your tools, sharpening your mind, or sharpening your body by instituting a daily or weekly regiment of successful practices that work. (By this I mean take time each day to learn your craft, read, or work out.)

**Learn your craft.** If you are in a digging slump, take a refresher course, ask someone for insight, or read articles and journals for new tips and techniques. If you are so inclined, join a forum related to your brand of potato digging. There are many groups or organizations online that you can connect with other potato diggers around the world and ask questions or share information.

**Know your potatoes.** You will get more potatoes by ultimately understanding the wants and needs of your potatoes. If your potato wants safety and security, then appeal to that. If they want something reliable, then appeal to that. Understanding them is the key to getting more potatoes to mash. If you are in tune with your potatoes, you will dig your way to a giant pot of mashed potatoes. If you don't know what makes them tick, then you will miss the mark every time and you will be staring down into an empty hole in the field.

**Follow RTS.** The RTS is "The Road to the Sale." Follow a specific sales process every time with your potatoes. Be a potato expert. Interview your potatoes to learn their wants and needs. Give a great enthusiastic demonstration or presentation based on those wants and needs. Write up your potatoes. No potato gets in your bag without writing up a sales slip. Close the bag. Don't let your potato get away. Overcome objecting potatoes and then follow-up with your potatoes. Make sure they are happy.

A successful potato digger knows to do all these things. When they run out of potatoes, they don't panic. They just do what they have been trained to do.

# Neglected Potatoes Will Rot

Tend to your potatoes. Follow-up. Keep in touch, and stay in front of them. If you just put them in the potato cellar and forget about them, they will go bad.

As a potato spoils it will start to shrivel up, and stink. When it rots and is left in the bag, it will spread to the other potatoes.

It is said that a happy potato tells one potato about their good experience. An unhappy potato will tell ten others about their bad experience. (I believe, with social media, it is more like three hundred.) Potatoes like to socialize online. They check review sites and will talk about us potato diggers. They will leave your fields in flocks if there is enough bad PR about your potato farm.

Likewise, if you try to diversify and do too many things (For example; if you tend to the corn, beans, squash, and peas at the same time) you will forget about your potatoes and they will spoil. Large black spots will form and they will start to stink. It affects the other potatoes and causes them to rot too.

Take care of your potatoes, and they will take care of you. Here are some ways you can take care of your potatoes:

**Institute potato hygiene**. a. Wash your potatoes often. Their skins have dirt residue on them from digging them up—no one likes to bite into a potato skin with dirt on it. b. Peel them before you boil them. (Unless you like skins in your mashed potatoes. Then refer to a. so you don't get dirt in your mashed potatoes.) Don't forget, Potatoes like to be taken care of and no one likes to eat dirt. Create a newsletter, keep them up to date, and engaged with the goings on of your farm. Send a birthday card or anniversary card. (You want to be careful about holiday cards—there are many potato holidays and not all potatoes celebrate them.) Create a potato club. Give them coupons or offers that only those potatoes in the club get. Hold a special event and invite your club of potatoes over. Make them feel excited to come to the farm and bring other potatoes.

**Develop proper potato service skills.** How do the other people on the farm treat your potatoes? Are they rude to them, ignore them, or talk down to your potatoes because they are just dirty tubers? Or, are they pleasant, acknowledge them, or talk up to them?

Make sure your farms diggers know how special potatoes are to you and to the farm. Make sure they have a passion and enthusiasm for growing and digging new potatoes. Institute a three-foot rule: If a potato washes up and is lying on the topsoil, or is within three feet, stop and acknowledge the potato—they may want to get into your bag. Make sure all of your diggers know as much as you do about potato digging. Let them know not to talk down or demean a potato. They may think a potato doesn't know what they are talking about, but that may not be the case. Talk to potatoes intelligently—they may be smarter than you are. With the prevalence of the internet, they may have done a ton of research too. With that, they may have received some bad information on the internet. It is okay to educate them, but don't talk down to them, or have a preachy attitude towards them—it will offend them and they will leave and go to another farm.

**Monitor Potato Social Media and Potato Review sites.** There is nothing worse to the digger and his farm than an unsatisfied potato getting on social media, or review sites and airing their grievances to the world. If you don't have routine potato hygiene or proper potato service skills in place you will find that you will have more negative comments and reviews on your farm's online sites. Also, think about what those people are saying in public about you and the state of your farm. Those same potatoes who slam you online will be badmouthing you every opportunity they get.

**Engage with your potatoes.** Lean how they want to be treated. Hold potato clinics once a month, bi-monthly, or once a quarter for your potatoes to get together and learn more about your ongoing service, or new services you have. If you want to break out and find new potatoes, hold a focus group. Invite other types of potatoes you don't already have in your fields for dinner while you ask them questions and find out what makes them grow.

If you have an upset, potato listen to their grievance. Don't take their complaint personally, their perception is their reality. Find out what they want. Take care of that potato. I don't mean you have to give away the farm, but if it's within reason, give it to your potato or come to a mutually satisfying agreement, to keep them in your bag.

"But they are a really bad potato," you say.

You are right. There are really bad potatoes out there. Here is another quick note about bad potatoes; avoid the potatoes with a green tint to the skin they have a bitter flavor. These have been exposed to too much light and have developed a toxin, which can cause conditions like cramping, headaches, diarrhea, and fever.

Nobody likes a stinky, rotten, mushy potato or a green potato that causes those ailments. You have to ask yourself, "How desperate am I to keep a bad potato?" Be careful, they usually spoil other potatoes. Sometimes, like above, you can get something positive out of that potato by trimming away the brown spots. If you don't think you can salvage anything, fire them. Throw them away in the incinerator and never have anything to do with them again. You are in charge of your farm. You don't have to put up with a bunch of rotten potatoes.

Don't forget to ask yourself, what caused them to rot? Is it something you or your diggers are doing? Or, is it a one-off potato that you just don't need in your bag? There is a difference? The first kind is a problem of neglect that re-occurs because you and your diggers are not taking care of your potatoes. If you keep getting rid of your potatoes, you will end up with none at all. If it is a case of a one-off green potato, that is causing gastro intestinal trouble to your diggers and wreaking havoc with your happy potatoes, then it is just fine to set them to flames.

## Sales Is Mashed Potatoes

Don't forget to take great care of your potatoes, they will lead you to more potatoes. If you neglect them, your potatoes will rot and spread to others.

# Potatoes Remove Warts

Potatoes aren't just good for sustenance. They are good for other things too. A potato removes warts. What are warts? They are problems a potato digger develops. A good potato will take away all of your problems.

It is a "old folk remedy" that if you cut a potato in half, rub one-half of the cut face on your wart and bury it, your wart will go away.

What are warts that diggers encounter?

**Excuses.** Excuses are like rotten potatoes, everyone has one, and they stink. There is nothing worse than a digger with an excuse. "It is the weather," or "Those potatoes are just stupid!" Excuses are deflections for incompetence, or lack of work ethic. There is no line item on the bottom line of your business for excuses. Successful diggers know this and don't make excuses for poor digging performance.

# Sales Is Mashed Potatoes

**Blame.** Don't play the blame game. There are many diggers out there that say, "It is someone else's fault." and, "Other diggers didn't do this or that," or, "So-and-so dropped the shovel and didn't pick it up." A digger is accountable for their own actions, hard work, education, digging abilities, and persistence. Remember this, when you are pointing the finger at others, there are three other fingers pointing right back at you.

**Negativity.** Negative thoughts and downer attitudes spread like a bad case of the warts. You need to deal with your negativity and the negativity of your diggers quickly. It will spread and infect the whole farm. Change your mental state. Think positively and act positively. Encourage your diggers to do the same.

If you have warts, dig up a potato, cut it in half, and rub it on your excuses, blame, and negativity and throw it out of the field. Put your problems aside, stop making excuses, don't play the blame game, and think positively!

If it doesn't work the first time, do it again and again until your warts are gone.

You will get rid of your warts.

# Potato Blight And Other Factors

Life has its challenges, so does Potato digging. At some point in your career, you will be hit with the potato blight. Potato blight is an algae like fungi that causes a serious disease of potato tubers. In warm and wet conditions, it spreads rapidly and can devastate and destroy entire crops.

Potato blight happens to us all. If it hasn't happened to you yet—you are one of the lucky ones.

Blight is a natural occurrence and there isn't anything you can do to stop it. It will eventually make it to your fields. You can do some things to mitigate it and minimize its effects.

What can you do if you get the blight?

There are a few things you can do:

**Learn to recognize blight.** The first step is to realize that you have blight. If you recognize the infected tubers with dark patches of reddish brown beneath the skin, you can handle it quick and control it. If you don't recognize it or choose to ignore it, the blight will spread wildly out of control. Early stages of the blight are easily missed, and not all plants are affected at once. Many potato diggers keep digging and their potatoes quickly decay into a foul smelling mush. Or, their healthy tubers rot later when in storage. When you know you have a problem, you can deal with it and change or adapt to the situation.

**Face it head on.** Too many times when digger's fields get the blight they want to deny it is happening. They ignore it and hope it will go away. Don't put your head in the dirt. If you don't do anything the blight will spread and it will get worse. Face your challenges head on and you will overcome them.

**Be pro-active.** Spray fungicides. Fungicides are normally only used in a preventative manner. If you prepare for the blight and spray ahead of time you will have a chance the blight won't hit you. If you have a period with good harvests, you can be rest assured the blight is right around the corner. Prepare your diggers. Look for ways to keep the other potatoes from developing the blight.

One way to keep other tubers form becoming infected easily is to protect them and pile dirt or mulch around the stems of the potato plants. This makes it harder for the blight to spread to the tubers underground.

**Change it up.** If it isn't working right do something different—change your tactics. Pick a different kind of potato. Maybe the kind of potato you are going after is the kind that is hit by the blight easily. Look for different varieties when the market changes or plant field resistant varieties that will grow and thrive through the blight.

**Control your environment.** Blight develops at temperatures above 10 Celsius and 50 Fahrenheit or if the humidity is between 75% - 85% for two days or more. If you can control the environment within your fields, you can minimize how the blight affects you. Make sure your diggers are aware they need to take extra special care of the potatoes during a blight season. In a depressed market, those who do the best with their potatoes will make it through that depressed market.

**Make cuts.** Sometimes it is necessary to cut out the problems. To get rid of the pathogens you have to remove the foliage. If you are close to harvest, you can remove the canopy to prevent the potatoes from becoming infected. Not all potatoes will be saved, but with the right cutbacks, you can get through the blight and live for the next season.

**Replant.** If all else fails, replant. But first you must scrap everything you have grown and plant again. You have to remove the infection from the ground. Don't leave any infected potatoes in the ground. Also, don't let any volunteer plants form left over potatoes sprout. They can be a source of the blight returning. This may mean also getting a new set of diggers. The old ones may be carrying the blight on them.

As potato diggers, not only do we have to deal with bight but also there are multitudes of other challenges we have to face. Many of these factors are all out of your control but you can learn to develop persistence and get through them.

**Drought.** Sometimes your fields dry up. When this happens, you need to find different ways to irrigate. Get some outside help—bring in trucks of water to keep your plants growing. Adapt to the conditions—plant some drought tolerant potatoes. Whatever you do, you can get through the dry times if you are creative and resourceful.

**Floods.** Sometimes, when it rains it pours. Floods can be bad and floods can be good. Floods come and wash away your potatoes and you have no potatoes left. After the flood, you have to tidy up and re-plant. Many times floods bring abundance. The rushing waters uncover potatoes you didn't know you had. Other times they place new soil full of nutrients on the ground and your crops thrive and produce more than ever before.

**Pests.** Pests like to attack our potatoes and keep them from growing. As potato diggers there are a variety of pests, you may have to take care of. You may have a group of people that do not agree with how you do business or believe your product is inferior. They may picket or boycott you and your farm. You may have people online saying things about your business that is defamatory or not true. Often there are competitors that may play dirty and smear your good name in the mud. Whatever the case, these pests can be dealt with. Spray pesticide (positive marketing campaigns), or get a truckload of ladybugs (lawyers) to deal with them. Don't let pests ruin your farm.

As diggers, we need to learn how to manage through a series of drought, floods, and pestilence—they are a part of life and you can't control when they come after you or your potatoes, but you can learn to deal with it in a positive way.

How can you stay positive when you hit a slump and these entire things build up causing fear, anxiety, and stress?

## Sales Is Mashed Potatoes

**Slumps.** There are days where you will feel out of sort. You won't want to get out there and dig. You just want to stay at home and do nothing. Keep in mind you have to work through it. Then, when you do get a potato, it breaks any slump you were having. It gives you a little boost and hope to find another one. Remember, a potato leads to more potatoes.

**Fear.** Fear is your mind playing tricks with you. It is the voice inside telling you the negative things that might happen in the immediate future—then you believe it to be true. If all you do is go around thinking you will not find any potatoes—you will not find any potatoes. If you think that, all you will get is rotten potatoes—you will get rotten potatoes! Staying positive during a slump is the key to getting out of that slump. Likewise, when you are reaping bushel after bushel of potatoes you need to stay positive too. If you fear this good crop will run out—then this good crop will run out.

**Anxiety.** Along with fear, anxiety may build up inside you. You may develop worry or have uneasy feelings about the long-term future that manifest itself into restlessness, headache, fatigue, muscular tension, or problems in concentration that affect your potato digging. When our fears build to a point they create anxiety that alters our mood. Many potato diggers develop excessive worry over their potato digging results. This worry can become irrational and often uncontrollable. This causes the potato digger's thoughts to become cloudy and their judgment to become impaired. We all know that bad decisions can ruin a potato digger. Anxiety over potato digging may cause you to want to withdraw or give up. If you are experiencing anxiety over potato digging, you may need to get some help managing your negative thoughts and maladaptive behaviors.

**Stress.** Along with fear and anxiety comes stress. A potato digger can take on many duties in their potato-digging career and can cause stress. Also, dealing with blight, daily problems, or managing a slump can be very stressful and can build tension inside and come out in various ways. Anger, impatience, moodiness, irritability, agitation, loneliness, depression, and isolation are a few manifestations of stress. Stress can affect many potato diggers. It is a hard business and isn't meant for everyone. You have to be tough and, as described above, you have to deal with many factors of potato digging on a daily basis and sometimes many times throughout a day. It can be somewhat overwhelming at times and stress is one of those things that can break a potato digger.

So, how do you deal with the stresses of potato digging?

You can control the source of your stress. Whether it be your boss or other potato diggers—talk with them about what is going on and see if there is a way to change the situation that is causing you stress. Also, you can learn to sometimes say "no" to adding more duties on your plate. Or, you can manage your stress outside of potato digging. Take a break, listen to music, work out, take a walk, or find some kind of hobby that helps you mentally or physically decompress.

A successful potato digger knows how to deal with all these things. They manage their fears, anxiety from their mistakes, and know how to move on. They don't gloat or fanaticize on past plentiful yields of potatoes. The past is the past. Today is today. Focus on your digging efforts "in the now' and you will be able to minimize fear and anxiety. Find a way to decompress and you will be able to manage your stress.

On top of all of this, a good potato digger doesn't bring potato digging home with them. They don't let a bad day in the field ruin their family life or interfere with their rest and relaxation time. In addition to that, they take a

# Sales Is Mashed Potatoes

break from work and enjoy life and its offerings outside of potato digging. Isn't taking vacations, going on trips, or staying home to relax what you are working for anyway?

Expect some rotten potatoes—days where you dig up nothing good. Do those days affect how you feel? No. Successful potato diggers don't let a few rotten potatoes get to them. Brown spots, blight, and other factors are just challenges to overcome.

Ride the blight out.

Manage through drought and floods.

Handle pests.

Control yourself and your thoughts.

Put forth the effort today.

Experienced potato diggers know that if they do all of these things, it will work out for the best.

# The One With The Most Potatoes Wins!

At the end of the day, it all comes down to who has the most potatoes and who has the biggest pot of mashed potatoes.

Now, there is always going to be X # of potatoes in the marketplace at any given time. The question you have to ask yourself is, "How am I going to get a bigger share?"

There are several things you can do daily to increase your share of potatoes. They are:

**Enthusiasm.** Enthusiasm is a boundless or intense positive emotion. Enthusiasm is contagious and it spreads quickly. Likewise, negativity spreads just as quick. Potatoes sense these emotional states. If you are constantly in a state of enthusiasm, your potatoes will notice that and will be drawn towards you. If you are in a constant state of negativity, your potatoes will be repelled. The most successful potato diggers know this and they check their level of enthusiasm often. They know how to turn their negative thoughts off and turn on the enthusiasm because they know that enthusiasm attracts and negativism repels.

**Persistence.** Great potato diggers never give up. They keep going despite the challenges they face. They are full of tenacity and have a relentless pursuit towards their goals (finding potatoes.) They are dogged workers and when faced with adversity they don't roll over and give up. They know inside that their hard work will pay off and if they keep digging, they will eventually find the mother lode of potatoes.

**Hard work.** Good potato diggers know that they have to roll up their sleeves and do the things needed to be successful and get potatoes in their bag. They are willing to do the things that other potato diggers aren't willing to do. Their work ethic is what sets them apart from other, less successful, potato diggers.

**Smarts.** On top of hard work, the best potato diggers work smart. They possess the mental acuity to out-think a potato in any situation. They are ready for any challenge that comes their way and are prepared for any objection that may come up.

**Luck.** Sometimes all you need is a bit of luck. Many potato diggers get lucky, but luck comes and goes. It is not constant. Don't hope to be lucky, prepare yourself to be successful and you will get lucky

**Preparation.** The most successful potato diggers look like they are lucky. Luck doesn't have anything to do with it. Their luck is purely preparation. They prepare to have enthusiasm. They prepare to persist. They prepare to work hard. They prepare to be smart and outwit. They prepare for success.

When you are prepared to do what you need to do daily, you will have more mashed potatoes than the other potato diggers out there and you will have all the mashed potatoes you need.

# Don't Become
# A Lazy Digger

We all know about couch potatoes. But what about couch diggers? They are the lazy, unworthy, shortcutting, good-for-nothing procrastinating diggers out there. They are a disgrace to hard working professional potato diggers.

Why is it that the lazy ones seem to get all the breaks? Why do they find big potatoes now and again while the hard working, ethical potato diggers seem to find only small potatoes? There is no rhyme or reason in the potato-digging world.

In the end, the lazy undeserving diggers meet their demise. They eventually self destruct while the hard working persistent diggers eventually find success and build up an empire of loyal and repeat potatoes. The lazy ones that rely on conquest potatoes end up running out of luck.

What happens when you focus on the big potato, work only one kind of potato, don't weed or manage your fields, or don't re-plant?

You eventually run out of potatoes!

There are lots of lazy diggers out there. Don't become a lazy digger!

Being a potato digger is fun. It is an exhilarating job. It is full of risk and reward. It is hard but easy at the same time. Follow your passion, and become a great potato digger at heart. If you are really good at it, it will be very lucrative. You can build a good life living on mashed potatoes!

How bad do you want it?

# Keep digging!

# For More Visit:

# www.LifeWorkElements.com

Business. Coaching. Goals. Inspiration.
Motivation. Persistence. Sales. Success. Training.
Elements For Your Life's Work

# About The Author

Tim Northburg is an author of several fiction novels as well as multiple sales training and motivational guidebooks. His motivational books help people discover simple truths so they can live happy, fun, and successful lives. Tim Northburg lives in colorful Colorado, at the base of the Rocky Mountains, with his wife and three daughters and enjoys writing non-fiction and fiction books of all kinds. He thrives on sharing his philosophy of success and motivation with others and he hopes his impact as a writer is thought provoking and fun. It is his long-term goal to inspire everyone to follow their dreams and achieve success in their lives.